NARCISSUS POETICUS By Steven Michael Pape

"And now it is time that I laid aside, at least for a few hours a day the world that pours in here from the outside."

- May Sarton (Journal of a solitude)

Dedicated to Patricia Roe,
'Our Pat'
28th March 1943-28th Jan 2022.

The light you left shines bright,
The memories remain, always.

Fly high, sleep well.
Peace & Love
X

Published by

**QUEENS   BROOKLYN   LONDON
ROME   SAN FRANCISCO**

TABLE OF CONTENTS

This World And Body.

This world and body,
Changing, aging,
The flow of life,
Rearranging.
The birth of the young,
The death of the old,
A constant change,
All life is controlled.
It's in the trees,
Centuries they stand,
It's in the earth,
You hold in your hand.
It's held in the eyes,
A knowing glance,
It's held deep within,
All life's a chance.
It's the slow decay,
That we know will come,
It's mistakes we've made,
That can't be undone.
The uncertainty,
That we know will rise,
It's thoughts we held,
Once deep inside.
It's the air we breathe,
As the sun does find,
This world and body,
All here beside.

***

<u>Towards The Light</u>

We head towards the light,
On a rattling train
Craning our necks,
Our heads out the windows
Like children on a day trip,
Curious tourists, a discovery,
Holding hands like young lovers,
Through tunnels
Awash with graffiti,
That reminds us of brighter days.
Below us tainted tracks,
The lost souls remembered,
By flowers, destroyed, discarded,
In memory of those who searched,
But just couldn't find.
Behind us is the past,
Left like discarded litter
Ahead is the future, unravelling,
The light comes into our view,
Like the new sun rising,
A startling light burning,
Our tear ducts, opening,
Happiness, descending,
We let them travel,
Into our smiling mouths.

***

<u>I Know You Can't See Me</u>

I know you can't see me,
But believe me I'm here,
Holding your hand,
Relieving you of your fear.

My arms round your shoulders,
I try to stop your tears,
I sit with you at night,
To try and soothe your fears.

I stand right before you,
Studying your face,
Seeing the beauty,
That I once helped create.

I look round your house,
At my picture on the wall,
Of when I was much younger,
And standing so tall.

You see, physically i'm gone,
But spiritually i'm here,
My presence is too strong,
To completely disappear.

My soul is in your soul,
Always entwined,
It's in every last sentence,
Every word, left behind.

If you could see where I went,
You would not believe,
The people i've met,
On our memories, we feed.

If you feel a presence,
Please open your mind,
Do not be afraid,
It's only me by your side.

I'm your spiritual guide,
I try to keep you safe,
As you travel this earth,
Moving from place to place.

My presence will strengthen,
Or that's what i'm told,
So I can go from invisible,
To something quite bold.

I'm the moon and the stars,
The wind and the rain,
The rising sunshine,
The day brings once again.

***

<u>Love Lays</u>

Love lays,
Like the waves crash,
The spray on our backs.
Love lays,
Like a bullet,
Too fast to react.
Love lays,
Like the Summer,
Skin glowing & red.
Love lays,
Like the insomniac,
Eyes open in bed.
Love lays,
Like the rain,
Cleansing our souls.
Love lays,
Like a creature,
Devouring us whole.
Love lays,
Like a fire,
As heat intensifies.
Love lays,
Like the strange,
Kaleidoscope eyes.
Love lays,
Like the excesses,
Party people, wild.
Love lays,
Like the long lost,
Now reconciled.

Love lays,
Like the Mother,
Cradling her young.
Love lays,
Like the music,
The songs we have sung.
Love lays,
Like the bed sheets,
Tangled, unmade.
Love lays,
Like the thoughts,
The memories we've saved.

***

<u>We Pick Leaves</u>

We pick leaves off the garden,
That the Autumn wind swirls,
Mixing the colours,
That nature unfurled.

The trees are half naked,
Like skeleton hands,
It's colourful protector,
Lying now on the land.

They crunch under our feet,
So fragile, and dry,
As from the sky
Even more do now fly.

And we study the shapes,
The veins that run through,
That once clung to life,
Like all of us do.

The wind is so cold,
It waters our eyes,
As Autumn shows us,
Her vibrant surprise.

The leaves in a pile,
The brown, red, orange, green,
The yellowing ones,
That we've only just seen.

Autumn is watching,
We sense that she sees,
The pile we've collected,
Moving in the breeze.

<u>Photos Of A Young Man</u>

There's beauty in the sepia,
The way the shadows fall,
Photos of a young man,
Staring at us from the wall.

Not a line etched on the skin,
Not a greying in the hair,
The eyes looking mischievous,
The way they always were.

A lifetime of discovery,
Is what still lay ahead,
The words still to be spoken,
And those that were left unsaid.

The Army uniform,
Stark against the light,
Portraying a true Gentleman,
Before he went off to fight.

And throughout his life,
He would recount his dreams,
All the horrors of the war,
And the thing's he had seen.

The sacrifices he had made,
The way he had to fight,
This photo is pride of place,
Illuminated by candlelight.

***

The Sun Beats Down

The sun beats down on weary faces,
As January departs bringing a new phase,
Ushering in a new chapter, a fresh page,
We devour the new sun like prisoners
Released from our inner solitude,
An alien concept, a surprising transition.
Surveying the garden, the disarray,
Caused by natures cruellest months,
In our minds eye we plan the next step,
The muddy boots and blackened nails,
Spades digging the dirty earth,
Snowdrops heralding the Spring,
The Daffodils rising with their colour,
Birds feeding on much softer ground,
The sky a lighter shade of blue,
All the clouds unscathed, not scarred,
Clean oxygen for the senses, the masses,
The sun taking the cold out of our bones,
Weary eyes surveying the landscape.
Hoping.

***

Sunday Dog Walk

The streets on a Sunday,
Quieter than the previous days.
Where people exited shops,
Laden down with alcoholic escapes
To blot out the working week,
The number crunching numbness.
The boss they'd like to kill,
Ever decreasing wages,
Poverty on the paper.
People ensconced in houses,
A warm cocoon of safety
And hot water heating,
The television glaring light
Onto rain streaked windows.
From one house a game show
Expectant contestants,
Audiences that applaud to order
Three doors down are showing
A classic film from the 80's,
Plucked from a dusty D.I.Y shelf
To relive a long lost childhood.
On the grass verges litter lays,
Crushed up cans and crisp packets,
Small tied up bags like presents,
That will never be reopened.
The streets patched with tarmac,
Like a band-aid on an open vein
The noise of nails and paws
Echoing down the wet slope.
Reaching the safe sanctuary of home,
Plastic window sills dirty with grit,
Vomited on from passing traffic,
The bulb inside flickering,
That I forgot to change.

***

The First Clear Day

The first clear day,
Heralding the Spring, perhaps?
From my vantage point,
A lone yellow flower
Protruding out of the cloying earth,
The petals, fragile in perfection.
The sun although shallow
Breathes a sigh of relief
A brief respite from the rain
A small glimpse of warmth.
We envisage the Summer
Those warm afternoons
Of relaxed contentment
The garden a quiet sanctuary
A serenity of the senses.
But, for now we are content
Albeit for a small minute
But it's there just showing us
Shining though weakly
All is not lost, brighter spells,
The first clear day to arrive
Showing us that it's still there
The sun although weak beating down
On pale faces, hopeful yet sick,
Wishing for the new dawn
To lead us onward
Into a collective sigh,
Of warmth and paddling pools.

***

<u>'Nice Day For A Funeral?'</u>

'Nice day for a funeral?'
This Spoken by a man
In an ill fitting top-hat,
And a starched Mourning suit,
Pressed like cardboard.
It was his shoes which annoyed me,
Polished to a high degree shine
Like pebbles coated with rain
They would of better befitted,
The person lying in the elongated car
Encased in an oak panelled box
(with removable brass handles).
The type of shoes business execs wear
To pretentious ceremonies,
Where acid etched awards
With their name adorned await.
A mantelpiece talking point
For their fake, dead eyed friends.
But I digress.....
And so I plaster on a forced smile
And look up to the blue sky
As if I'm pondering his words
'A nice day for a funeral?'
What a ridiculous thing to say.

***

<u>Pale Sun</u>

Pale in the Morning sun,
Blinking like newborns.
Our tone alabaster,
Like the statues we saw,
In old art documentaries.
The sun although weak,
Seems to energise us,
Banishing the tiredness,
That earlier consumed.
And as the birds now sing,
A chorus from brittle branches,
We inhale, meditate,
The sun stark against the white,
Like polished marble.

****

<u>Spring Awakening</u>

Spring awakening,
Showing herself
Underneath the broken fences,
Brittle wood like parchment
Battered by storms Ciara & Dennis,
Leaving debris strewn recklessly
Across the sodden grass,
Old rusty nails like nicotine teeth
In an old weathered face.
Out of the decay & chaos
Flowers protrude under the wood
Vibrant Lillies bold in colour,
Daffodils as bright as the sun
Breaking through with strength
Leaving us with the hope,
Of regeneration, of regrowth,
Spring introduces herself, awakening,
The only way she can, with colour.

***

<u>Breathe Planet</u>

Breathe planet,
The roads devoid of cars,
That damaged your lungs,
Like cheap illegal cigars.

Breathe planet,
The sky is again yours,
No longer scarred by the trails,
As the aeroplanes roared.

Breathe planet,
Now the streets are so empty,
That once littered your backyard,
With their plastic, their debris.

Breathe planet,
Let your rivers become clean,
As the animals return,
To how it once had been.

Breathe planet,
Let your rain wash away,
The evidence of our footprints,
That we leave behind everyday.

Breathe planet,
Let the birdsong ring true,
As we sit and reflect,
On all the damage we do.

Breathe planet,
Let your oxygen rise,
As we sit locked inside,
Staring up at your sky.

***

I Hold Them Inside

I hold them inside my beating heart,
Remembering the good times,
And the many sad years apart,
The inscribed stone,
A fresh bunch of lilies,
I talk through the earth,
On every single visit.
Leaving incense smouldering,
Into the Autumn breeze,
Transcending my thoughts,
That disappear with the wind,
Past the resting places,
Of God's little babes,
The windmills & teddies,
That distraught Parents have made,
Through the ornate gates,
Where so many have passed,
Past the statues and crosses,
That were built to last.
All of us with the memories,
That where there at the start,
We'll always hold these thoughts,
Inside our beating hearts.

****

Autumn Invites Us

Autumn invites us,
The leaves on the pavement.
The rain sticks them down,
In an abstract arrangement.

The mornings are dark,
As we climb from our beds
Several layers of clothes,
A warm hat on our heads.

There's beauty in decay,
All the colours on show
Nature dying with dignity,
In it's Autumnal flow.

We walk with our heads down
The cold rain in our eyes
Yet everyday it is changing,
Everyday's a surprise.

Yet when the rain ceases,
We take a chance to look up
At the differing colours,
That now fall from above.

Its nature dying with colour,
As it now sheds every leaf
Leaving a bare skeleton,
Now devoid of its sheaf.

A kaleidoscope of colours,
That the trees now present
Autumn invites us,
To its graceful lament.

***

<u>Even Though You're Gone</u>

Even though you're gone
Your face shines
In my unconscious,
Your voice an echo
In my deep dreams,
A slumber of confusion
Your scent an illusion
That arrives like
A spring flower
Slowly forming
The shadows & shapes
No longer a figment
Of my imagination
More a message
A calling,
Telling me you never left.

***

<u>Halo</u>

I still check
On your sleeping form
As I have from your beginning.
Even though you're grown,
And now into double figures.
I listen to your slumber,
Unintelligible words,
A childhood dream
Innocence entwined.
I cover you up, contained,
In a blanket, soft with comfort,
A kiss softly on your cheek
Checking your breathing,
That you are resting safely,
And move your hair
Out of your eyes
Trying not to misplace,
Your halo.

***

<u>This House</u>

This house,
Breathing its dust
And inspiration,
From its wooden floors,
An element of nature inside,
Its Victorian architecture
The vast space of time
The memories remain,
Embedded into foundations,
Creeping,
Into my cobweb brain.
And the shadows
That caress the corners,
Watchful eyes,
Guiding me forward,
To spiritual growth
To more expression,
Purity in the words,
Tighter structure.
To be truthful,
With no hint of regret.
I'll leave my old notebook,
Battered and torn,
Unintelligible notes
In a secret location,
For the future to find.

***

This Garden

This garden,
Where creation grows.
The life and death,
Before our eyes
From nothingness,
To colour, and back again.
An endless cycle of growth.
We plunge our hands
Into the recesses of the earth,
Deep into the dark bowels,
Pulling out the intestines
The dead roots of yesterday.

***

<u>In The Morning</u>

In the Morning,
Awaking to Autumnal dark
The rain a crescendo,
Beating on the window panes.
Lying prone under the bed sheets,
Too catatonic to move,
Every movement taking energy.
As outside, traffic noise,
Cars taking occupants
To their working places
The tired eyes moving
In slow unison,
With the windscreen wipers.
The morning breath,
Shaking off last nights,
Excesses, the late memories,
Of an early Morning embrace,
The alarm call vibrating,
Like lost lovers consoling.

****

<u>Nature Accepts</u>

Nature accepts,
The birth and the decay.
The trees shedding leaves
Leaving them naked, vulnerable.
The earth digesting the debris,
Like greedy vultures
Feeding the roots,
Hidden in the deep recesses.
The branches, brittle,
Are still home for the bird's,
As they sway precariously
In the morning breeze.
The tree's like all of nature,
Accept this brief death,
Knowing that as they sleep,
They will soon once again rise.

****

<u>When The Rain Stops</u>

When the rain stops,
After a five day downpour,
That invaded our soul,
That drenched, diluted thoughts,

That made us eager to stay,
Locked behind our own doors,
Cold seeping into bones,
Water trickling down our necks.

Turning gardens into swimming pools,
Drowning flowers where they stood,
The weeds grow in abandonment,
Bright green and climbing.

When the sun does arrive,
It's like a light in a dark room,
A switch pressed behind the sun,
Illuminating the decay that's left.

The flowers rise up, eyes open,
The colour and clarity shines,
As the sky changes from black,
To a subtle shade of blue.

***

<u>I Woke</u>

I woke to the sun on the daffodils,
Highlighted in the kitchen window
Vibrant with the light illuminated,
Each one like miniature suns.
Their pungent odour, enveloping,
The early morning room
Mixing in with the scent,
Of freshly brewed coffee
From their vantage point,
A view of the garden
The stretching green plus,
Two trees, one trimmed down,
The other standing tall
Bare branches rising upwards,
Pigeons nestling in the air.
Whilst on the ground,
Sparrows and blackbirds
Peck hungrily at the earth
Eating the grass seeds
That I layed yesterday,
A luxurious breakfast I'm sure.

****

<u>We Laugh Like Children</u>

We laugh like children,
To banish our adult minds
Albeit for a brief moment.
As we swing into the air
Fit our aching bodies
Onto a slide not designed,
For our shapes.
In these times we transgress
Back into our childhood,
The adult world far behind.
The laughter sounding strange
To our unaccustomed ears
We feel lighter, more human,
Our empathy mixing,
With the feeling of freedom
We are transported back
Into our earlier times
Where our only worries
Was the sun going down
Our jumpers once goalposts,
Now adorned in the cold
The dark, a signal to go home.
***

<u>Understanding</u>

Until we remember the,
Nurturing in our souls
Divinity in our minds
Empathy in our hearts
Realising all our dreams
Standing by our beliefs
Truth in our words
Acceptance of our mistakes
Nature under our feet
Daylight in our eyes
Infinite in our wisdom
Noting of all our thoughts
Growing into ourselves.
***

<u>I Wait</u>

I wait....
After weeks of no words,
No inspiration/ideas
No paper traces,
Lying lost.
Where the hum-drum,
Of life, the frantic rat-race
Has corroded my mind,
Leaving me briefly
Like an automation
A body but no mind.
I wait....
For the lost, tranquil days,
Of pacing through nature
Observing growth and decay,
Both intertwined
Where the earth and I
Combine together
To create beauty.
I wait, hopeful,
As I've always known
That patience is a virtue
That inspiration will arrive
Sparking my psyche
Words flowing too fast
For my hands to follow
Paper strewn carelessly
Notes and dictations
As it all comes together
Like long lost lovers
Caressing.

***

<u>Valentine's</u>

Carrying the Valentine's flowers
Perched precariously in my arm,
Fighting against the wind and rain
Trying somehow to protect them.
Passing the early morning walkers,
The brave, panting joggers,
Who glance up at the burst of light
Nestled in the crook of my elbow,
Balanced like a newborn.
I cut the stems, place in a vase,
On the windowsill they shine,
The sun lighting up their colours,
Their aroma filling the room.
Over the next few weeks I observe,
As they slowly wither,
As the petals crumble to my touch,
Slowing dying, yet with dignity,
A touch of colour still remaining.

****

<u>Waterfall</u>

You are heard,
Before you are seen,
The cascading water,
A noise so serene.

Ebbing and growing,
The foam soon subsides,
A cleansing of the soul,
A place for us to hide.

An anger, uncontrolled,
Nature's natural flow,
Breaking over the rocks,
A sight to bestow.

Purity in your passion,
The stream that lies beneath,
Visible in the water,
The flowing Autumn leaves.
***

<u>The Serenity Of The Senses</u>

Memorial plaques on oak stained benches
And the afternoon chorus of birds
Lovers stroll arm in arm, embraced,
Over ice cream cones and sun cream smears.

We all seem oblivious to each other
In this haven of tranquillity
Devoid of the fog fumes of life
A gothic house deep in the forest
Dead vines climb over the entrance.

I envisage the long halls, the vastness,
Plateaus of forgotten delicacies
As off the lake the sun beats down
Like a blinding torpedo of light.

It stings our unaccustomed eyes
As swans in their natural habitat
Greedily indulge in stale bread
Brought by human creatures.

Bicycles and the crunch of gravel
Children play, the noise deafening
Breaking the silence, freedom roams,
We feel air on our tired, pale faces.

Lethargic on legs used to hard pavements
Over the hill we climb, uneven paths,
It alters the way we walk
A time now to appreciate and stroll
Through the ambience of green.
***

Ever-Changing

Ever-Changing,
Out here.
As I throw aside the inertia
Here, beside nature.
Where the earth dwells,
And small creatures emerge.
The vastness, the empty spaces,
Like a blank canvas,
That a lone artist devours.
I notice indiscretions,
In the earth, the garden,
The structures that surround
All are easily remedied.
The flowers though can't be saved
Their brief cycle ending,
A last respite of colour
Before they sleep again
Cocooned in the earth
Safe for another year,
To be replaced
By the ever-changing,
Colour and beauty
That catches the morning sun,
In a perfect cascade.
The bitter tang of earth
That the mild wind carries
Into the recesses of my being,
A new beginning, I wait patiently.

<u>The still of the afternoon</u>

Birds singing in the still of the afternoon
The cherry red-breast as Robins scoot
Across the soil, pecking up food,
That's been discarded from the feeders
Positioned high up in the trees.
And the wrens, although small in size
Ring out a loud pitched siren sound,
That doesn't depict their stature.
Blackbirds solitary by nature,
Their own company a reward
Feed as the sun highlights their dark hues.
All of creation, strong willed servants,
The survival instinct intertwined
In the most basic of methods.
An afternoon of chorus sounds,
Echoing through a sunlit garden.
  ****

<u>Come sit with me</u>

Come sit with me
As the sun slowly sets
At this table.
These chairs arranged,
To accommodate bodies.
Where idle chatter,
Mixes in with the chorus of birds
And the traffic from the street
Creates a strange crescendo
A hypnotic ambience,
Where we shrug off the problems
That life tries to create
And instead bask in the afterglow
Of the English garden.
The sun warming up
Our ailing bodies,
Our struggling senses
Repairing our consciousness
That the day tried to destroy.

<u>Freedom</u>

Freedom is in the mind,
In the way we perceive
It's also in the eyes,
In the things that we see.

Freedom is found in nature,
In the flowers and the trees
The influx of wildlife,
The birds and the bees.

Freedom is roaming,
Over a carpet of green
Studying what's around us,
Like it's never been seen.

Freedom is in the sun,
That lights up our faces
It's around every corner,
It lies in various places.

Freedom is in the rain,
The clouds that are bruised
In the rainbow that follows,
Vibrantly casting its hues.

Freedom is in the wind,
That transports our dreams
The howling of its voice,
The anger as it screams.

Freedom is in the snow,
So pure and untouched
And now in the footprints,
That turns it to slush.

Freedom is in the beholder,
Freeing the shackles of the mind
Freedom is right before you,
If you seek, you will find.
****

<u>**We Will Remember**</u>

We will remember,
As our Grandchildren ask,
These years that we lived
Their questions from class.

And we'll recount it all,
To disillusioned eyes
All of our memories
We'll tell of the times,

Where hugging was forbidden,
And paranoia ruled
Where we listened to lies,
Portrayed by the fools.

As we recognised our friends,
Only by their eyes
As their faces were obscured,
By a mask like disguise.

Where the television spoke,
And told us what to do
Where any truth told,
Was only spoken by the few.

And our house was a prison,
Our freedom was work!,
As we fought through the boredom,
With a laugh and a smirk.

And we homeschooled our Children,
With our limited designs
We where teachers for a while,
Although we prayed to resign.

Where the public rebelled,
They'd scream and they'd shout
Whilst the enemies in blue,
With batons they'd clout.

And freedom of speech,
Would be a whitewash of shame
The only questions they'd ask,
Would be, 'What is your name?'

And we very nearly lost it,
Our heads were a mess,
A political propaganda,
Putting our sanity to the test.

The rules and regulations,
Where all driving us mad,
Altering our moods,
From happy to sad.

But through all this darkness,
We saw a beacon of light,
A hand held out before us,
To rescue us from our plight.

And our Grandchildren will listen,
Everything now recalled,
As we recount our memories,
We will remember it all.
***

<u>English Roses</u>

Yesterday there was nothing,
Just several small buds bursting,
Like a corset too tight to contain.
Today, English roses red,
Crafted like art in the night hours,
Vibrant in the early morning sun.
Clinging to the foliage
Spray painted by nature,
Burning like fire,
Each petal, perfect,
The scent illuminating
The sight empowering,
Warming to the new day,
Welcoming the first sighting,
Showing her beauty,
Like a new beginning, exposed,
Naked like a newborn.
The sun highlighted,
Onto every single petal.
***

<u>Observe</u>

Can you see us?
We softly ask,
That lone walking man,
Who treads the green path
Always observing,
With a furrowed brow,
The sun in his eyes,
Refreshing the dry earth.
Will he notice our arrival?.
Our colour and vibrancy?
The change from green to yellow?
The show we've developed,
From growth, to our birth,
Come closer,
Caress and smile at us,
And as you finally recognise
The change in surroundings,
And marvel as you forget,
The inner world you inhabit.
Come closer still,
Smell our sweet scent.
We've been dead for a year,
Awaiting your presence,
But we have risen, briefly,
For your pleasure, your eyes,
The beauty you see,
Is the beauty you feel inside,
Our gift to you.
Observe.

<u>This Sacred Place</u>

This sacred place,
That i briefly visit
In certain seasons.
As inner voices, beckon,
And guide me towards.
A place where no one asks,
What i am doing?
Why i am here?.
A place where one sits,
On freshly cut grass
Where incense smoke,
Lazily mixes with summer breeze.
My thoughts transgressive,
A sacred place,
Where i touch the stone surface
And trace each letter, inscribed,
With my hand,
Where warm lips kiss cold,
And flowers are arranged,
In impressive formations.
And the ancient angels
With watchful eyes
And weathered bodies,
Observe my exit.

<u>Autumn Acquiesce</u>

Summer's almost gone,
As the trees flutter protection
Onto the ground
Leaving a shroud of colour.
As we shiver into blankets,
And central heated rooms,
Creak with new surroundings.
The crisp, early mornings,
The long forgotten jumpers,
The plumes from tired mouths,
But the colours that she shows,
Bright burning red leaves,
Subtle shades of yellow, orange,
Nature leaving her mark,
The message in her dying,
This beauty that surrounds,
Autumn acquiesces.
Accepting the inevitable,
Inviting the change.

<u>Under Blue Skies</u>

Under blue skies
Where the sunflowers sing,
And the freshly trimmed grass,
Sticks to our bare souls.
And as the sun highlights
The beauty, the imperfections,
Skin pale like the statues
We once observed,
On a cold Winter's day,
Clouded in our cocoon
Our words mere plumes,
As thoughts transcend.
Now under blue skies,
As perfect as fresh snow,
That we ruined by our imprints,
Our vivid footsteps.
The table moist with dew,
That cements each page,
Diluting each sentence,
An ink-stained daydream desire.
And the Buddha's watchful,
Observing the illusion,
The sun blinding the eyes,
That once could see.

Goodbye To Nature

I bid goodbye to nature,
Albeit for today,
As I cross the plush grass
That earlier was a warm carpet,
Now a cold compress.
As statues are alighted,
Buddhas serene and still,
Watchful eyes, thoughtful.
Flowers that spewed beauty
Now asleep, yet illuminated,
By a cheap warm white,
Solar light.
And the trees stretching
Into the night sky, caressing,
The broken veined beauty,
A caricature of skeleton hands,
Outstretched, inviting,
My final goodbye,
Is to walk to the door,
As the late bird sirens,
Echo their tired goodnights,
I close the door,
Letting nature and I sleep.

<u>Street Scene</u>

Graffiti tags, faded, diluted,
Washed by the rain,
Dirty, polluted.
People scrape ice,
From car windscreens,
And shake their heads,
Of forgotten dreams.
The workers don't walk,
But just amble along,
Their ears are full,
Of musical song,
To drown out the noise,
That their brain replays,
Another shift, another day.
Dogs are walked,
At this ungodly time,
Many pavements,
And hills to climb.
Buses roll past,
All masks and eyes,
Hiding the mouths,
And the yawns demise.
The shops are open,
Selling red top rags,
Spewing their lies,
Into recycling bags.
The Mornings cold,
And black as tar,
The journeys endless,
It seems too far.
But all of us,
Still with hopes and dreams,
A tired collective,
Walking this street scene.

<u>In this drawer</u>

In this drawer
Faces peer out
Reviving memories
Before the last light.

On this cardboard
Where memories belong
Be it a favourite poem
Or a well known song.

These memories remain
Deep in our hearts
As our dearly beloved
Bring light to dark.

And we've sat and held
This two-page sheet
Tried to hide the sadness
Underneath.

And relived the good times
Conversations we've shared
The hugs and the kisses
The way which they cared.

And as the music plays out
For their final lament
All of us are remember
This love that they Sent.

<u>'Our Pat'</u>

You had a heart made of gold
Always helping everyone
That sentiment still remains
Even though you're gone.

Raising all your children
With dignity & respect
The life lessons you taught them
Is one they'll never forget.

And every person you met
You did so with a bright smile
That would light up the room
And stretch for many miles.

And those hugs that you gave
That warmth so deep inside
Helped every single person
That your arms entwined.

And when you arrive
On the heavenly plain
There'll be some many people
Calling out your name.

And that smile we remember
That's etched in our minds
Will now be displayed
To those that you find.

Dedicated to Patricia Roe, 'Our Pat'
 28th March 1943-28th Jan 2022.

ABOUT THE AUTHOR

Steven Michael Pape was born in 1974 in Ilkeston, Derbyshire, England.

A prolific reader and writer from an early age he soon focused on poetry and the different forms and structures he could achieve through this medium.

In 2009 Pape released his debut book, 'The Awakening Soul' and the following year released it's companion, 'Escapism' both books contained dark gothic poetry a theme which Pape soon distanced himself from writing, although later poems would contain dark imagery these were more focused on society and it's issues.

Pape is also a regular contributor to FM's quarterly anthology featuring worldwide poets, as well as having his poems published in several papers, forums and magazines.

'**Narcissus Poeticus**' is his tenth book and is his most mature, structured, and honest work to date.

<u>OTHER WORKS</u>
<u>By the same Author:</u>

The Awakening Soul (2009)
Escapism (2010)
Observations With Half-Closed Eyes (2011)
A Closed Mind Is An Open Trap (2012)
21st Century Wasteland (2013)
This Fragile Life (2015)
Life In The Past Frame (2016)
A Weapon Called The Word (2018)
Inner Voices: 3AM Poems (2019)

Steven
As Editor: (Anthologies)
Landscape Of The Dream (2010)
The Art Of Darkness (2011)